I0190173

Horses

Ashley Lee

Explore other books at:
WWW.ENGAGEBOOKS.COM

VANCOUVER, B.C.

e WWW.ENGAGEBOOKS.COM

Horses: Level 1
Animals That Make a Difference!
Lee, Ashley 1995 –
Text © 2021 Engage Books

Edited by: A.R. Roumanis
and Lauren Dick

Text set in Arial Regular.
Chapter headings set in Arial Black.

FIRST EDITION / FIRST PRINTING

LIBRARY AND ARCHIVES CANADA CATALOGUING IN PUBLICATION

Title: Animals That Make a Difference: Horses Level 1
Names: Lee, Ashley, author.

Identifiers: Canadiana (print) 20200309684 | Canadiana (ebook) 20200309692
ISBN 978-1-77437-697-3 (hardcover)
ISBN 978-1-77437-698-0 (softcover)
ISBN 978-1-77437-699-7 (pdf)
ISBN 978-1-77437-700-0 (epub)
ISBN 978-1-77437-701-7 (kindle)

Subjects:
LCSH: Horses—Juvenile literature
LCSH: Human-animal relationships—Juvenile literature

Classification: LCC SF302 .L44 2020 | DDC J636.1—DC23

Contents

What Are Horses?

Horses are big, strong animals.

Horses have lived with humans for thousands of years.

What Do Horses Look Like?

Shires are the tallest horses. They are about 6.6 feet (2 meters) tall. The smallest horses are miniature horses. They are less than 3.3 feet (1 meter) tall.

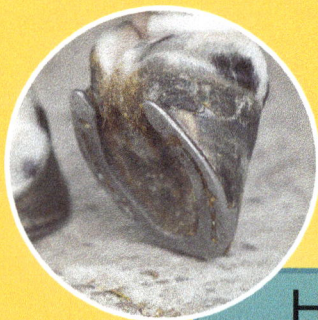

Horses' feet are protected by a hard nail called a hoof.

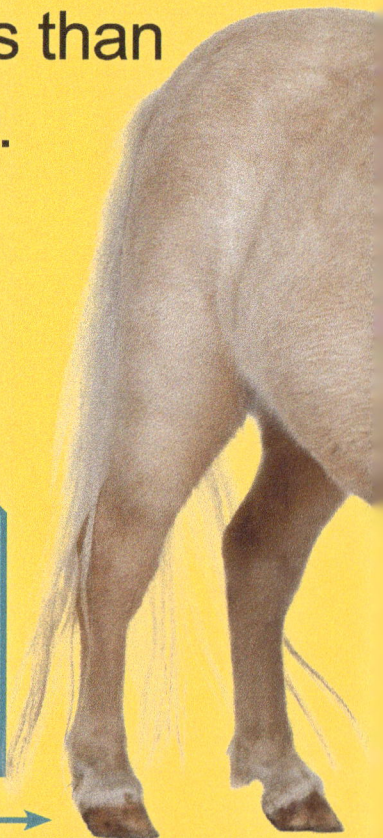

Horses have long hair on their necks called a mane.

Horses have large teeth. A horse's age can be guessed by looking at its teeth.

Where Do Horses Live?

Many horses live on farms. They sleep in a stable. Some horses live in the wild. They sleep outside.

Clydesdales are large horses that come from Scotland. Hanovarians are strong horses that come from Germany. Paso fino horses come from Puerto Rico.

Scotland

Europe

Atlantic Ocean

North America

Asia

Africa

Germany

Peurto Rico

Pacific Ocean

N

Legend
- Land
- Ocean

0   2,000 miles

0   4,000 kilometers

Southern Ocean

Antarctica

9

What Do Horses Eat?

All horses eat grass. Horses on farms also eat grain and hay.

Horses spend up to 17 hours eating grass every day.

How Do Horses Talk to Each Other?

Horses make many different sounds. They will neigh, whinny, or snort. People can tell what horses are feeling by looking at their ears.

A horse with its ears back is angry.

Horses are curious when their ears face forward.

Horses often make a snorting sound when they are excited.

Horse Life Cycle

Baby horses are
called foals.

One-year-old
horses are
called yearlings.

Horses become adults when they are 4 years old.

They live for 20 to 30 years.

Curious Facts About Horses

The fastest known horse ran at a speed of 55 miles (88 kilometers) per hour.

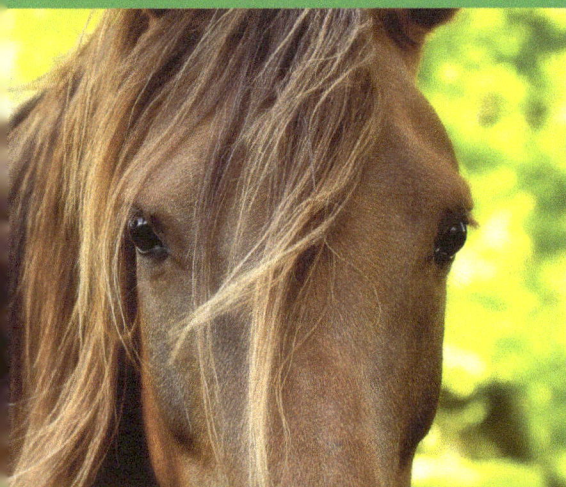

A horse's eyes can see in two different directions at once.

Horses can sleep standing up.

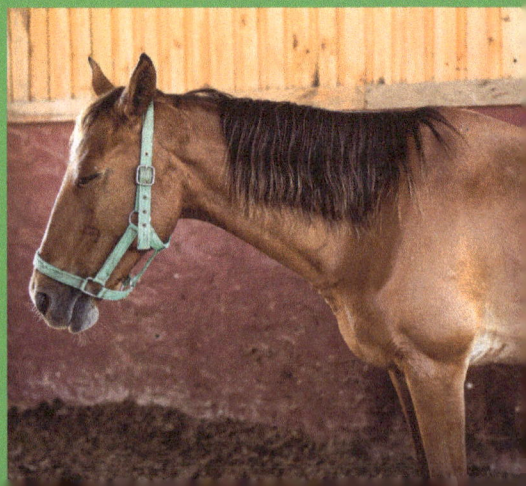

Horses cannot breathe through their mouths. They only breathe through their noses.

Horses make about 10 gallons (37 litres) of saliva every day.

A horse can see behind itself without turning its head.

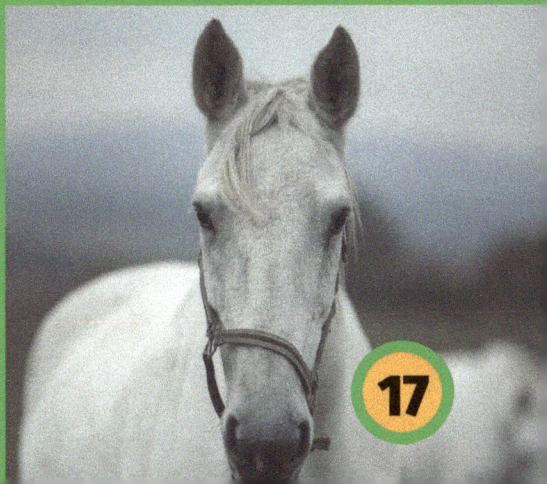

Kinds of Horses

Horses are related to zebras and donkeys. There are around 200 different kinds of horses. These are split into three groups.

Draft horses are used for carrying heavy farm loads.

Light horses are
used for riding.

Ponies are the smallest
horses. They are gentle
and do not get tired easily.

How Horses Help Earth

Many kinds of energy
are harmful to Earth.

Horse manure can be turned into energy. This kind of energy does not harm Earth.

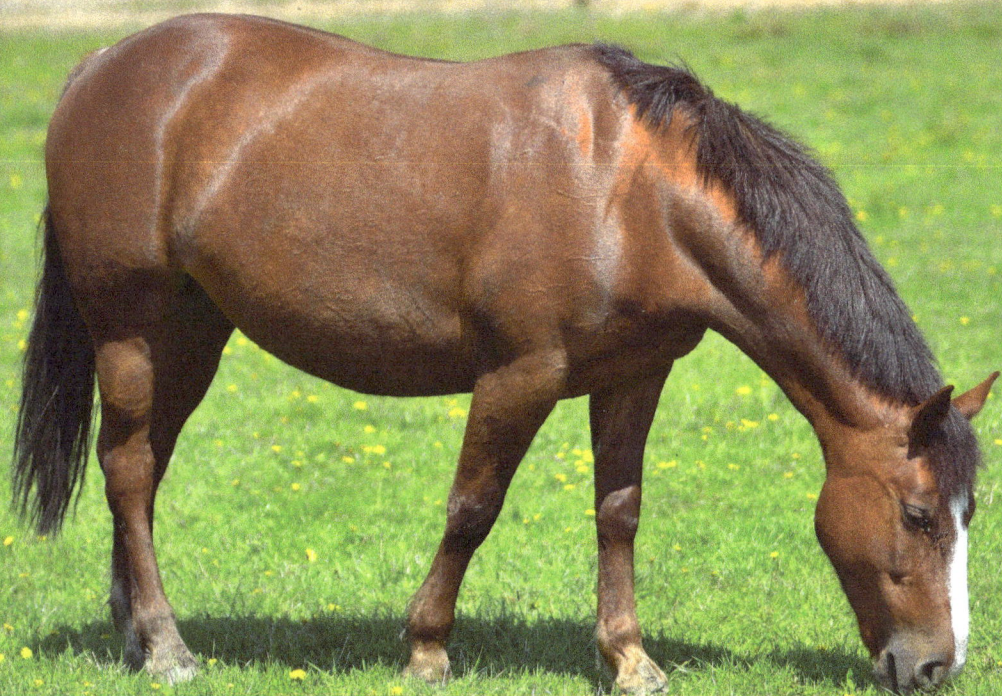

How Horses Help Other Animals

Wild horses break the ice on lakes and rivers in winter.

This gives smaller animals a place to drink. Many animals are not heavy enough to break through ice.

How Horses Help Humans

Horses help farmers
carry heavy supplies.

Police horses are used in places like Canada. They help keep people safe.

Horses in Danger

Some horses are endangered. This means there are very few of them left.

Dales ponies were once used for carrying heavy loads. They are disappearing because machines are now used to carry heavy objects instead.

27

How To Help Horses

Taking care of horses can cost a lot of money. Owners have to pay for their food and visits from the vet.

Many people take horse riding lessons to help support horses. This is also a great way to learn more about horses.

Quiz

Test your knowledge of horses by answering the following questions. The questions are based on what you have read in this book. The answers are listed on the bottom of the next page.

1 What is the long hair on a horse's neck called?

2 How long do horses spend eating every day?

3 How long do horses live?

4 What are horses related to?

5 What can horse manure be turned into?

6 How do horses help farmers?

Explore other books in the Animals That Make a Difference series.

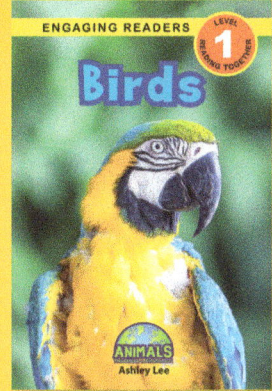

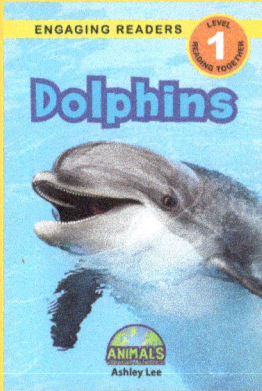

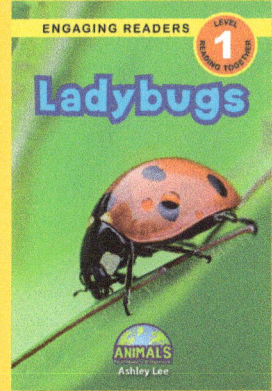

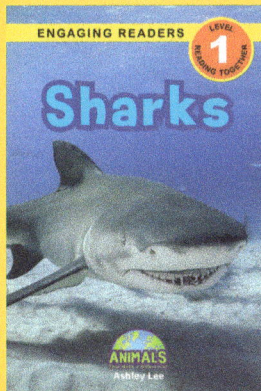

ENGAGING READERS — LEVEL 1 — **Bees**
ENGAGING READERS — LEVEL 1 — **Bats**
ENGAGING READERS — LEVEL 1 — **Birds**

ENGAGING READERS — LEVEL 1 — **Dolphins**
ENGAGING READERS — LEVEL 1 — **Horses**
ENGAGING READERS — LEVEL 1 — **Ladybugs**

ENGAGING READERS — LEVEL 1 — **Pigs**
ENGAGING READERS — LEVEL 1 — **Sharks**
ENGAGING READERS — LEVEL 1 — **Squirrels**

Visit www.engagebooks.com to explore more Engaging Readers.

Answers:
1. A mane 2. Up to 17 hours 3. 20 to 30 years 4. Zebras and donkeys 5. Energy 6. By carrying heavy supplies

www.ingramcontent.com/pod-product-compliance
Lightning Source LLC
Chambersburg PA
CBHW040227040426
42331CB00039B/3414